I0569202

Catalogue of permanent circulation coin and paper money types

Volume III

Switzerland (1850-2016)

Catalogue of permanent circulation coin and paper money types. Volume III. Switzerland (1850-2016)

by H G M Eggenkamp-Vlaanderen

©2016, Dr HGM Eggenkamp-Vlaanderen

ISBN 978-90-816059-9-1 (Soft cover)

Onderzoek & Beleving, Bussum, The Netherlands

post@onderzoek-en-beleving.nl

Catalogue of permanent circulation coin and paper money types

Volume III

Switzerland (1850-2016)

H. G. M. Eggenkamp-Vlaanderen

1st edition, 2016

Preface

The period of modern numismatics (since about 1800) is perhaps the most interesting ever. Within this period different types of monetary standards (silver, gold, bimetallic) alternated, and periods of sometimes impressive inflation occurred, in many countries even resulting in hyperinflation. The period after World War II even is the first period in the Earth's history that continuing inflation is the norm. It also is the period that paper money took over as the main appearance of circulating currency money. This started towards the end of the 19th century, when gold coins were mostly stored in vaults and gold coin equivalents started to circulate primarily in the form of banknotes. This became especially important during World Wars I and II when silver and gold coins were hoarded and were replaced by different kinds of paper money in circulation. After World War II no longer circulation gold coins were issued anymore and in most countries even silver coins disappeared from circulation in the years after World War II. As a result at this moment coins are solely "small change" in most countries while paper money is used for larger payments. Of course only when payment is made in currency and not taking into account the plastic and even "telephone" money that is increasingly becoming more important. In most countries the trend is that more and more of the payments are done by electronic means, so that the importance of currency for payment has decreased and it is expected to continue to decrease considerably in the near future.

In this series of books it is aimed to classify the different appearances of currency money (both coins and different types of paper and polymer money) in one system. The reason is that I believe it is necessary to look at both appearances to understand the circulation of money in a society. In most current catalogues coins and paper money are treated separate or it is even necessary to acquire different catalogues for coins and for paper money. In fact, the collection of coins and the collection of paper money are very often even considered as different fields of collection and many people either collect coins or collect paper money. However, during the lifetime to a certain denomination coins and paper money series can easily alternate. For example in Switzerland, silver coins disappeared from circulation in 1914 due to hoarding at the start of World War I. They were replaced by the various treasury notes from 1914, as well as the only 5 Franken note that was ever issued. After the war was over the treasury notes could be withdrawn, and although the 5 Franken note continued to be issued until 1952 it was never replaced by a second issue and as such it was the only 5 Franken note that was ever issued by the Swiss National Bank. This history is just one example and to understand the circulation of money in a country it is necessary to understand how coins and paper money did alternate in history.

What I (personally) consider a problem for the collector of circulation coins is the increased issue of different kinds of commemorative coins. Especially after about 1980 the number of commemorative coins increased in many countries to such an extend that the regular circulation coins, the coins that the public on the street actually uses in commerce, are hardly visible in the major catalogues. It is one of the reasons that I prepared this catalogue and the main reason that only very little information on commemorative coins is provided. They are mentioned if they comply to circulation specification and if they are issued in relatively large quantities at face value. But without images which are provided solely for the regular permanent types.

The currency described in this series is classified according to a newly developed classification scheme. This scheme is built as a hierarchical system based on i) the nominal value, ii) the year a new coin or note series is issued for the first time, iii) the year of issue and iv) if more than one variety is issued in one year an indication of these varieties. In the case a redenomination or a monetary reform takes place the new currency unit is fit into the old one. For example, the old Franc in France has been replaced by the new Franc, at a ration of 100:1, in 1959. As the nominal value in the classification does not change the new Franc will get the same nominal value at the first hierarchical level as the old 100 Franc. This way it is hoped that historical continuity is shown properly in the series presented in these catalogues.

This series of catalogues has been prepared with mainly one collector/numismatist in mind, notably myself. I was already looking for the "ideal" catalogue for a while, and in my opinion it seemed that this was not available. For that reason I decided that I should prepare this catalogue myself. This series, of which this is the third volume and of which hopefully several more will be produced, is the result of this endeavour.

It is hoped that this series of type catalogues will fill the gap that exists for people that are mostly (or even only) interested in circulation coins, or people that want to learn about the combined history of the currency, both in metal or paper form. They will get an overview of actually used currency in a country, and get a (good) impression of the money the really circulated between all people.

Hans Eggenkamp-Vlaanderen

Introduction to the series

Each volume in this series describes the circulating currency, that is the coins and paper money that circulate in a certain, more or less defined area, in most volumes a single country. This may seem vague, and the reason is that it is aimed to classify the circulating money in a way that shows the continuity of the money in a region over a longer timespan, mostly from the early 19th century until the present day. In several countries that means that significant political changes have happened, and this is generally reflected in the money that circulated in that specific country. Well known examples are countries that were colonised during the 19th century and became independent during the 20th, as well as countries that were occupied for longer or shorter periods during the last two centuries. Also mergers and split-ups of countries are reflected in the circulating currency. An example of colonisation and subsequent independence will be Indonesia, where the coins and notes of the Dutch East Indies will be incorporated as this was the name of Indonesia before its independence. More complex histories are shown in the cases of central Europe (for example Austria-Hungary and its successor states) where significant territorial changes have occurred after World War I and during World War II as well as after the collapse of communist eastern Europe. Important examples in this region are the former Yugoslavia and Russia/former Soviet Union.

Apart from this there are several differences between the major well known catalogues and this catalogue series. It is clearly not a prize catalogue. So at no place indications are given concerning the values of the coins or banknotes to collectors. I believe there is no real need to supply values as these are easily traceable on various specialised internet sites such as Ebay.com, Catawiki.com and Numista.com. And these values are by definition more up to date than values in a printed catalogue. For the same reason no attempt have been made to discuss the grade of the coins and paper money types. The images presented are not necessary of high quality specimens and sometimes they even are of specimens of only the quality "good" depending on the quality of my personal specimen.

The catalogue aims at presenting, a what I would call, a "scientific" classification of the coins and paper money series and types, including a "scientific" way of giving references for each series and type. Although I tried to add images for as many as possible coins and paper money types (at least concerning the "permanent" types) not all have been pictured. The reason is that I do not have pictures of all permanent types. Most coins are images from specimens present in my personal collection. 19th century line drawings are taken from contemporary books which are mostly available from Google books. Bank notes are either scans from my personal collection or obtained from websites from Central Banks after consultation with the relevant division. In some cases images were even made available by the issuing bank. No commemorative coins and banknotes are pictured in this series of catalogues. As written before one of the main reasons for writing this catalogue series is the fact that commemoratives are taking too much space in many modern catalogues and render the regular circulating coins and notes more and more invisible. Some commemorative series are mentioned however, if the issue limits are are large and if they are issued at face value, so that at least a small chance existed that they were used in commerce. However, no images are supplied. As this catalogue is a "type" catalogue the individual mintage years for coins and years, dates and signature combinations for paper money are not mentioned.

Acknowledgements

I would like to express my gratitude to the Swiss National Bank for giving me permission to reproduce banknote images from their website and supplying me with images of Series 8 and 9 banknotes. I would also like to thank the Swiss mint for giving permission to reproduce the gold coin images from their website. I would very much like to thank my wife, Nina Vlaanderen-Eggenkamp, for her support and patience in writing this catalogue, teaching me how to make photographs of coins and her help in correcting the final text of this catalogue.

Table of Contents

Switzerland

Switzerland is a confederation of 23 cantons in central Europe, most of it in the western Alps. It is a democratic country with a surface (land) area of 39,973 km^2 and an estimated population of about 8,121,830 people in July 2015.

Map of Switzerland showing the main cities (image from CIA The World Factbook)

Location of Switzerland within Europe (image from CIA The World Factbook)

In this catalogue I describe the Swiss coins issued since 1850 and paper money (banknotes) issued since 1907. The coins and paper money are classified in this catalogue following a newly developed method. Before 1850 the monetary situation in Switzerland was extremely complex as all cantons (subdivisions of the country) had the right to issue their own money. Although during the period that Switserland, as the Helvetic Republic, had a unified monetary standard from 1798 until 1803 the cantons regained the right to issue their own money after 1803. As also foreign coins circulated in the country it is estimated that towards 1850 about 8000 different coins (and early banknotes) circulated in the country. In 1848 it was decided that only the confederation would have the right to issue coins and in 1850 the first national coinage was issued. All older Swiss and foreign coins were then demonetised. Paper money was however not yet issued nationwide and the number of issuing banks was over 50 in the middle of the 19th century. It was only in 1874 that a comprehensive revision of the Federal Constitution regulated that the Confederation is authorised to pass legislation governing the issue and redemption of banknotes. In 1891 this resulted in a regulation in the Federal Constitution, whereby the banknote monopoly would be transferred to the Confederation. Finally in 1905 legislation to form a National Bank (National Bank Act) was passed and this bank started to issue nationwide banknotes in 1907. Earlier banknotes were subsequently removed from circulation. As the 1907 banknotes from the Swiss National Bank were the first that were issued for the whole country only banknotes from this and later issues are incorporated in this catalogue.

The following coins and notes are incorporated in this catalogue. Circulating coin series issued at face value since 1850, all banknotes issued by "Schweizerische Nationalbank" since 1907 and treasury notes issued by the Federal Treasury in 1914 and currency notes issued by the State Loan Bank of the Swiss Federation in 1914. This includes the commemorative coins issued at face value in large quantities, which however are not depicted in this catalogue. This indicates that coin series solely consisting of commemorative coins only have an indication of type and size and the period that they were issued. Not incorporated are commemorative coins issued issued above face value only in small mintages and banknotes that were not issued to the general public because they were only printed as reserve notes. The gold 25 and 50 Franken coins minted between 1955 and 1959 are mentioned in this catalogue as they are very well known to exist. Although they were never issued because the gold price rose above face value before they could be issued, they are also considered as real Swiss, potentially circulating, coins considering the interesting article about them on the website from the Swiss Mint (http://www.swissmint.ch/d/downloads/dokumentation/nu mis_beri/25-50-FR-GOLDMUENZEN.pdf). Their mintage figures were high and they were, unlike the reserve banknotes, initially certainly minted to circulate.

In the period since 1850 Switzerland used only one currency unit. In 1850 the Swiss Franken was adopted with the same characteristics as the French Franc. This currency unit still exists and it can be considered as the most stable currency that has existed during the last two centuries worldwide. Each Franken is divided in 100 Rappen. Switzerland has four national languages and both the currency unit and the subdivisions have different names in each of these four languages. In German the main unit is called "Franken" and the subdivision "rappen", in French they are called "Franc" and "centimes", in Italian "Franco" and "centesimo" and in Romanch "Franc" and "Rap". As German is the most spoken language in Switzerland (by about 63.5% of the population) in this catalogue the German names are used, so "Franken" and "rappen". Both units are the same in singular and plural, so it is (for example) one Franken and 5 rappen. In German all nouns are written with a capital letter, however, in this catalogue series we use a capitalised word for the main currency unit and non-capitalised words for the subunits. This usage will also be applied in this volume so that we use "Franken" for the main currency unit and "rappen" for the subunit.

In this catalogue only coins and banknotes that were issued (in principle) in the whole country are classified. These are the coins issued by the treasury of the Swiss Confederation which have on the obverse the text (in Latin) "HELVETIA" together with a female representation, a coat of arms (either complete or just the cross), or a depiction of a shepherd (on 5 Franken coins only; Swissmint, 2008). Most people believe that this is a depiction of Wilhelm Tell, the famous legendary Swiss freedom fighter, but officially it just is a shepherd. On the reverse a short indication of the value in the form of a number in the case of values below ½ Franken and the value with the abbreviation "Fr." for values from ½ Franken and higher. Because Switzerland is a country with four national languages it was considered most appropriate to use Latin as the language for the legends on the circulating coins. Paper money that is classified is issued by the Swiss National Bank ("Schweizerische Nationalbank" in German, Banque Nationale Suisse" in French, "Banca Nazionale Svizzera" in Italian or "Banca Naziunala Svizra" in Romansh). The name of the national bank is added in each of the four national languages on modern banknotes. The Swiss National Bank issues banknotes only since 1907, so banknotes are only described from that year. Apart from the Swiss National Bank issues during World War I the treasury also issued currency notes and these are described too.

Classification system

The classification developed for this book series uses a hierarchical system as described below.

I) The first level is based on the logarithm (base 10) of the nominal values of the coins and paper money that is issued in the country. This is determined by taking the logarithm of the nominal value, add the lowest number to get a positive result, multiply by 10 and put a "O" before. For example the lowest denomination in Switzerland is the one Rappen/centime coin (CHF 0.01), the logarithm is -2.0, to make it positive 2 is added (so that the result is 0.0) then it is multiplied by 10 (so as to get 0) then a leading 0 (zero) and an "O" is added in front and a slash at the end (so that the general code for "one Rappen" is "O00/"). In this system the Franken main currency unit gets the code "O20/".

ii) The second level indicates the actual coin or note series. A coin series is a series of coins issued according to a defined nominal value and well defined technical specifications that include (at least) metal composition, coin shape, weight and diameter. Note series are defined less strict but mostly by the nominal value, the design (a small change indicates a note within the same series, a completely new design defines a new note series) the size and the composition of the note. The series are defined (classified) by the first year that a coin or note series is either minted, authorised or issued. This depends on the information that is readily available. For coin series it is the year that is normally accepted as the first year a coin is officially minted. This is the year that in most catalogues is accepted as the first year of mintage. This is not necessarily a year with a high mintage. For note series this is the year that the note is authorised, and that is printed on the note. This year is in many cases a few years before the note was actually issued. After the year either a "C" or an "N" is added to indicate if the series is a coin or a note series.

iii) The third level indicates the year that an individual coin or note is minted or issued as indicated on the note or coin. For coins this is the mintage year as indicated on the coin. For notes the system is necessarily more complicated. On notes issued in Switzerland two different systems were used. On early notes (up to series 5) each print run had a separate date that was printed on the note, later notes (from series 6) have the year that they are printed as part of the serial number. The first two digits of the serial number indicate the year that the note was printed.

iv) At the final level the variability with a coin or note series is indicated. For standard circulation coins this exist of a capital letter for common obverse and reverse sides. A big change in the design is indicated by a different letter, small variations in the design by a superscript number. Different issues of the same obverse/reverse combinations in a year (such as coins minted at different mints) are indicated by small letters after the design indications. Commemorative coins are indicated with a "Z" at this level. When more commemoratives are issued in one year followed by a superscript number. If either the obverse of the reverse of a commemorative coin is of a standard design this is indicated at this level too. In this catalogue however no commemorative designs are described as it is a "permanent types" catalogue. In the case of banknotes at this level the different signature variations issued within a year series are distinguished using lower case letters.

Set-up of the catalogue

In the following pages the coins and paper money series that circulated in Switzerland are presented. Starting from the lowest nominal value (the rappen) until the highest nominal value (the 1000 Franken banknote). Within each nominal value a short summary is given of the series (either coins or notes) that were issued and an indication is given of the period that a certain nominal value was circulating in the country. After this introduction a table is presented that shows the various coin and note series, including the years these were issued (first year and last year, not all years within this range may exist on actual coins or notes), the composition, the mass, the diameter and the thickness in the case of coins. The composition is given with the name of the alloy and the percentage of the various metal present in the alloy. The metals present in alloys of Swiss coins are: Au (gold), Ag (silver), Cu (copper), Ni (nickel), Zn (zinc), Sn (tin) and Al (aluminium). In the case of paper money series only the size is given. No attempts have been made to show the weight or the thickness of the paper money series. This table gives a good impression how coins and paper money series alternated for each nominal value.

Then a section is written for each coin or paper money series. For each coin series after the title a figure is available that shows the exact size of the coin. As paper money normally has a size that is larger than the size of a page in this book for paper money this is not given. This figure is followed by images and short descriptions of the obverse and reverse types. Coins are all presented at the same size (1 inch, 2.54 cm), paper money issues are presented at identical widths of 1.8 inch or 4.57 cm, while the height depends on the actual width to height ratio of the represented note. Finally a table is presented that indicates the various coin or paper money types (possible obverse-reverse combinations) and the years that these combinations were issued (again, first year and last year, not all years within this range may exist on actual coins or notes). In the case of coins cross references are given with the major world coin catalogues (KM#, Standard Catalog of World Coins by CL Krause and C Mischler; S# Weltmunzkatalog 19. Jahrhundert by G Schön und H Kahn, and 20. und 21. Jahrhundert by G Schön und G. Schön and Y# A Catalog of Modern World Coins 1850-1964 by RS Yeoman). In the case of paper money a cross reference is given with the P# from the Standard Catalog of World Paper Money by A Pick (3rd edition 1980) for older issues or the 9th and 16th edition of this catalogue for modern issues (notes that were issued since 1961) now written by N Shafer and GS Cuhaj. Finally an empty column with "X" in the title is presented in which the owner can indicate whether a specimen of the coin or paper money type is present in his or her own collection. The presence of commemorative coins in the coin series is roughly mentioned with the years they were issued, but no further descriptions or information is given.

Coin and note image credits

The images of the coins and paper money described in this publication are taken from three different sources. The majority of coin photographs (silver, bronze and zinc coins) are specimens from the author's collection. Images from most gold coins are taken (with permission) from the Swissmint website, where these images are available for download. The banknotes are taken from the website from the Swiss National Bank. Images from banknotes from series 8 and 9 were supplied by the Swiss National Bank and they contain the required word SPECIMEN on the images. The designs of all coins are copyright Swissmint, the designs of all banknotes are copyright Swiss National Bank.

The catalogue

1. O00/ 1 rappen (CHF 0.01)

Minted from 1850 until 2006, after which it was removed from circulation due to inflation. Even long before 2006 the coin was not regularly seen in circulation as the production cost was up to four times larger than the nominal value of this coin. Issued as coins of two different types, one in bronze (1850-2006), one of the longest running coin series that has ever existed in the world(!) and one in zinc (1942-1946) issued during World War II to save on metals that were difficult to obtain during these years even for a neutral country like Switzerland.

Series	Years	Comp.	Mass (g)	Size (mm)	THK (mm)
O00/1850C	1850-2006	Bronze (95% Cu, 4% Sn, 1% Zn)	1.5	16	0.8
O00/1942C	1942-1946	Zinc (100% Zn)	1.2	16	0.8

1.1. O00/1850C Bronze 1 rappen coin (1850-2006)

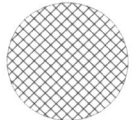

This, probably the longest serving coin series that was ever in use (156 years), was issued with only two obverse and reverse designs, until World War II with a classic design, and after that with a more modern design. The coins of the first design were demonetised on 1 February 1952, the coins of the second design on 1 January 2007.

Obverse A   *Obverse B*

Obverse A: Coat of Arms of Switzerland with freedom cap. Leafs to left and right. "HELVETIA" above and year below.

Obverse B: Swiss cross with "HELETIA" above and year below.

Reverse A   *Reverse B*

Reverse A: "1" with wreath around.

Reverse B: "1" with ear of wheat behind.

Type	Years	KM#	S#	Y#	X
O00/1850CyyyyAA	1850-1941	3	15	18	

Type	Years	KM#	S#	Y#	X
O00/1850CyyyyBB	1948-2006	46	41	54	

1.2. O00/1942C Zinc 1 rappen coin (1942-1946)

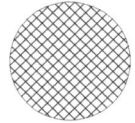

Issued during and until shortly after World War II to save on strategic metals. Only one design that is the same as the pre-war one rappen coins. These coins were demonetised on 1 February 1952.

Obverse   *Reverse*

Obverse: Coat of Arms of Switzerland with freedom cap. Leafs to left and right. "HELVETIA" above and year below.

Reverse: "1" with wreath around.

Type	Years	KM#	S#	Y#	X
O00/1942Cyyyy	1942-1946	3a	15a	18a	

2. O03/ 2 rappen (CHF 0.02)

Minted from 1850 until 1974. This coin was issued in fewer years than the 1 rappen coin and the mintage numbers were generally less than that coin. Apparently in 1974 it was decided that there was no need for this coin anymore and it was abolished and demonetised on 1 January 1978. Two bronze series were issued, as in 1932 the weight of the coin was increased to be twice as heavy as the 1 rappen coin. Like the 1 rappen denomination the 2 rappen denomination was minted in zinc during and briefly after World War II.

Series	Years	Comp.	Mass (g)	Size (mm)	THK (mm)
O03/1850C	1850-1931	Bronze (95% Cu, 4% Sn, 1% Zn)	2.5	20	0.9
O03/1932C	1932-1974	Bronze (95% Cu, 4% Sn, 1% Zn)	3.0	20	1.1
O10/1942C	1942-1946	Zinc (100% Zn)	2.4	20	1.1

2.1. O03/1850C Light bronze 2 rappen coin (1850-1931)

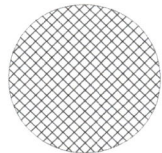

Issued with only one obverse and reverse design. Replaced with a heavier version in 1932. The coins of this series were demonetised together with the heavier and zinc 2 rappen coins on 1 February 1952.

Obverse   *Reverse*

Obverse: Coat of Arms of Switzerland with freedom cap. Leafs to left and right. "HELVETIA" above and year below.

Reverse: "2" with wreath around.

11

Type	Years	KM#	S#	Y#	X
O03/1850Cyyyy	1850-1931	4	16	19	

2.2. O03/1932C Heavy bronze 2 rappen coin (1932-1974)

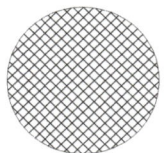

In 1932 the weight of the 2 rappen coin was increased to become twice as heavy as the 1 rappen coin. Except for the years in World War II this series was issued until 1974. The coins with the pre-war design were demonetised on 1 February 1952, the post-war coins were demonetised on 1 January 1978. Issued with two obverse and reverse designs, until World War II with the same design as O03/1850C, and from 1948 with a much modernised design.

Obverse A   *Obverse B*

Obverse A: Coat of Arms of Switzerland with freedom cap. Leafs to left and right. "HELVETIA" above and year below.

Obverse B: Swiss cross with "HELETIA" above and year below.

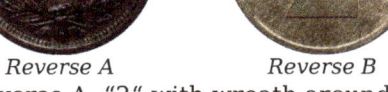

Reverse A   Reverse B

Reverse A: "2" with wreath around.

Reverse B: "2" with ear of wheat behind.

Type	Years	KM#	S#	Y#	X
O03/1932CyyyyAA	1932-1941	4	16	19	
O03/1932CyyyyBB	1948-1974	47	42	55	

2.3. O03/1942C Zinc 2 rappen coin (1942-1946)

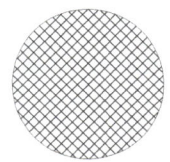

Issued during and until shortly after World War II to save on strategic metals. Only one design that is the same as the pre-war 2 rappen coins. These coins were demonetised on 1 February 1952.

Obverse   Reverse

Obverse: Coat of Arms of Switzerland with freedom cap. Leafs to left and right. "HELVETIA" above and year below.

Reverse: "2" with wreath around.

Type	Years	KM#	S#	Y#	X
O03/1942Cyyyy	1942-1946	4a	16a	19a	

3. O07/ 5 rappen (CHF 0.05)

Issued as coin since 1850. Originally as billon coin containing 5% silver, since 1879 in base metals only. The metal composition of these coins changed a few times, but the design has never really changed since it was first issued. Five series made of different metal compositions were issued since 1850.

Series	Years	Comp.	Mass (g)	Size (mm)	THK (mm)
O07/1850C	1850-1877	Billon (5% Ag, 60% Cu, 25% Zn, 10% Ni)	1.67	17.15	0.7
O07/1879C	1879-1890	Copper-nickel (75% Cu, 25% Ni)	1.8	17.15	0.9
O07/1918C	1918	Brass (60% Cu, 30% Zn)	1.8	17.15	1.0
O07/1932C	1932-1941	Nickel (100% Ni)	1.8	17.15	0.9
O07/1981C	1981-....	Aluminium-bronze (92% Cu, 6% Al, 2% Ni)	1.8	17.15	1.0

3.1. O07/1850C Billon 5 rappen coin (1850-1877)

When the Franken was introduced as national currency in Switzerland in 1850 it was decided that it would have the same value as the French Franc. To make the small change in silver meant that they would become very small coins, and for that reason it was decided to make them of billon, containing only a small amount of silver, only 5% in the case of the 5 rappen coin. Minted with only one design. Demonetised on 30 June 1886.

Obverse   *Reverse*

Obverse: Coat of Arms of Switzerland with ears of wheat on both sides. "HELVETIA" above and year below.

Reverse: "5" in centre with wreath around.

Type	Years	KM#	S#	Y#	X
O07/1850Cyyyy	1850-1877	5	17	20	

3.2. O07/1879C Copper-nickel 5 rappen coin (1879-1980)

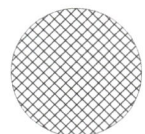

In 1879 the small amount of silver was removed from the 5 rappen coins and they were issued as copper-nickel coins. These coins continued to be in circulation until they were replaced by aluminium bronze coins in 1981 and were demonetised on 1 January 1984. In 1918 these coins were minted in brass, probably either due to high nickel prices during World War I or to save this metal for potential war efforts, and from 1932 until 1941 they were minted in nickel, apparently because the nickel prices were low enough during that period and the Swiss government aimed at using only one metal for all coins that were positioned between the bronze and the silver coins. This series was issued with only one design.

Obverse

Reverse

Obverse: Female head representing liberty, "CONFŒDERATIO HELVETICA" and year of mintage around.

Reverse: "5" in centre with wreath around.

Type	Years	KM#	S#	Y#	X
O07/1879Cyyyy	1877-1980	26	24	23	

3.3. O07/1918C Brass 5 rappen coin (1918)

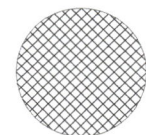

Issued in 1918 only with the same design as the copper-nickel 5 rappen coins. They were demonetised on 1 January 1924.

Obverse

Reverse

Obverse: Female head representing liberty, "CONFŒDERATIO HELVETICA" and year of mintage around.

Reverse: "5" in centre with wreath around.

Type	Years	KM#	S#	Y#	X
O07/1918Cyyyy	1918	26a	24a	23b	

3.4. O07/1932C Nickel 5 rappen coin (1932-1941)

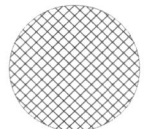

Issued between 1932 and 1941. Same design as the copper-nickel and brass 5 rappen coins. Demonetised, together with the copper-nickel 5 rappen coins, on 1 January 1984.

Obverse   *Reverse*

Obverse: Female head representing liberty, "CONFŒDERATIO HELVETICA" and year of mintage around.

Reverse: "5" in centre with wreath around.

Type	Years	KM#	S#	Y#	X
O07/1932Cyyyy	1932-1941	26b	24b	23a	

3.5. O07/1981C Aluminium-bronze 5 rappen coin (1981-....)

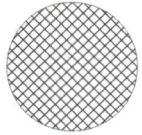

Issued since 1981. Still the same design as the older base metal 5 rappen coins.

Obverse   *Reverse*

Obverse: Female head representing liberty, "CONFŒDERATIO HELVETICA" and year of mintage around.

Reverse: "5" in centre with wreath around.

Type	Years	KM#	S#	Y#	X
O07/1981Cyyyy	1981-....	26c	24c		

4. O10/ 10 rappen (CHF 0.10)

Issued as coin since 1850. Originally as billon coin containing 10% silver, since 1879 in base metals only. In most years it was issued as a copper-nickel coin, only in 1918 and 1919 it was issued as brass coin and from 1932 until 1939 as pure nickel coin. These last coin series are no longer legal tender. All copper-nickel 10 rappen coins (issued since 1879) still are legal tender, and as such it is the longest running coin series on earth that is still issued with the same design as when it was first issued. A total of four 10 rappen coin series were issued, and just like to 5 rappen coins the design of the base metal series has never changed.

Series	Years	Comp.	Mass (g)	Size (mm)	THK (mm)
O07/1850C	1850-1876	Billon (10% Ag, 55% Cu, 25% Zn, 10% Ni)	2.5	19.15	0.9
O07/1879C	1879-....	Copper-nickel (75% Cu, 25% Ni)	3	19.15	1.2
O10/1918C	1918-1919	Brass (60% Cu, 40% Zn)	3	19.15	1.3
O07/1932C	1932-1939	Nickel (100% Ni)	3	19.15	1.2

4.1. O10/1850C Billon 10 rappen coin (1850-1876)

When the Franken was introduced as national currency in Switzerland in 1850 it was decided that it would have the same value as the French Franc. To make the small change in silver would mean that they would become very small coins, and for that reason it was decided to make them of billon, containing a small amount of silver, only 10% in the case of the 10 rappen coin. This coin was minted with only one design and it was demonetised on 30 June 1886.

Obverse   *Reverse*

Obverse: Coat of Arms of Switzerland with oak leaves around. "HELVETIA" above and year below.

Reverse: "10" in centre with wreath around.

Type	Years	KM#	S#	Y#	X
O10/1850Cyyyy	1850-1876	6	18	21	

4.2. O10/1879C Copper-nickel 10 rappen coin (1879-....)

In 1879 the 10 rappen coin was replaced with a copper-nickel version. This coin is currently, and even with the same design, still issued every year as small change in Switzerland. As a result this is the longest running coin series with only one design that has existed in modern numismatics.

Obverse   *Reverse*

Obverse: Female head representing liberty, "CONFŒDERATIO HELVETICA" and year of mintage around.

Reverse: "10" in centre of coin with wreath around.

Type	Years	KM#	S#	Y#	X
O10/1879Cyyyy	1879-....	27	25	24	

4.3. O10/1918C Brass 10 rappen coin (1918-1919)

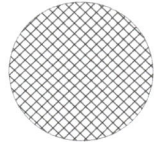

Issued for two years only at the close of World War I. The reason for issued this coin is most probably to same on the cost of nickel for minting coins. Same design as O10/1879 and can easily be recognised due to its yellow colour. It was demonetised on 1 January 1924.

Obverse *Reverse*

Obverse: Female head representing liberty, "CONFŒDERATIO HELVETICA" and year of mintage in legend.

Reverse: "10" in centre with wreath around.

Type	Years	KM#	S#	Y#	X
O10/1918Cyyyy	1918-1919	27a	25a	24b	

4.4. O10/1932C Nickel 10 rappen coin
(1932-1939)

Issued between 1932 and 1939. Same design as the copper-nickel and brass 10 rappen coins. This coin was demonetised on 1 January 2004.

Obverse   *Reverse*

Obverse: Female head representing liberty, "CONFŒDERATIO HELVETICA" and year of mintage around.

Reverse: "10" in centre with wreath around.

Type	Years	KM#	S#	Y#	X
O10/1932Cyyyy	1932-1939	27b	25b	24a	

5. O13/ 20 rappen (CHF 0.20)

Issued as coin since 1850. Originally as billon coin containing 15% silver, since 1881 as a pure nickel coin. Unlike the 5 and 10 rappen coins it was considered appropriate to use pure nickel for the 20 rappen coin as it was a more expensive metal. Since 1939 minted in copper-nickel just like the other small silver coloured coins. The 20 rappen was never issued as a brass coin. A total of three 20 rappen coin series were issued. The design of the pure nickel and the copper-nickel coin series has never changed and is still the same as in 1881.

Series	Years	Comp.	Mass (g)	Size (mm)	THK (mm)
O13/1850C	1850-1859	Billon (15% Ag, 50% Cu, 25% Zn, 10% Ni)	3.25	21.05	0.9
O13/1881C	1881-1938	Nickel (100% Ni)	4	21.05	1.3
O13/1939C	1939-....	Copper-nickel (75% Cu, 25% Ni)	4	21.05	1.3

5.1. O13/1850 Billon 20 rappen coin (1850-1859)

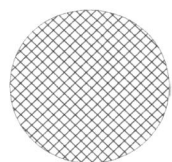

When the Franken was introduced as national currency in Switzerland in 1850 it was decided that it would have the same value as the French Franc. To make the small change in silver would mean that they would become very small coins, and for that reason it was decided to produce them in billon, containing a small amount of silver, only 15% in the case of the 20 rappen coin. This coin was minted with only one design. The billon coins were demonetised on 30 June 1886.

Obverse *Reverse*

Obverse: Coat of Arms of Switzerland with flowers around. "HELVETIA" above and year below.

Reverse: "20" in centre of coin with wreath around.

Type	Years	KM#	S#	Y#	X
O13/1580Cyyyy	1850-1859	7	19	22	

5.2. O13/1881C Nickel 20 rappen coin (1881-1938)

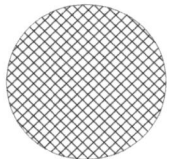

At the moment that silver was abolished from the billon coins it was decided that the 20 rappen coin could be minted in pure nickel in stead of copper-nickel. The reason was that a more valuable coin could be minted in a more expensive metal and that its metal value would be closer to the actual nominal value of the coin. Another advantage of nickel is that it is a very hard metal and that wear would be less than would be expected for the copper-nickel coins. Although these coins were no longer minted in pure nickel after 1938 they were legal tender until 1 January 2004. Only one design was used on coins from this series.

Obverse   *Reverse*

Obverse: Female head representing liberty, "CONFŒDERATIO HELVETICA" and year of mintage around.

Reverse: "20" in centre of coin with wreath around.

Type	Years	KM#	S#	Y#	X
O13/1881Cyyyy	1881-1938	26	20	25a	

5.3. O13/1939C Copper-nickel 20 rappen coin (1939-....)

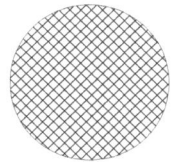

During the 1930s the small silver coloured coins (5, 10 and 20 rappen) all were issued in nickel. towards the end of this decade it was decided to move to copper-nickel coins, what would mean that the 5 and 10 rappen coins would revert to their original composition and that the 20 rappen coins would change for the first time to that composition. The 20 rappen coins were the first to move to a copper-nickel composition in 1939. 10 and 5 rappen coins followed in 1940, although 5 rappen coins were for one more year (1941) made in pure nickel before they were finally minted in copper-nickel again. The design of the copper-nickel 20 rappen coins continued to be same as on the pure nickel coins.

Obverse   *Reverse*

Obverse: Female head representing liberty, "CONFŒDERATIO HELVETICA" and year of mintage around.

Reverse: "20" in centre of coin with wreath around.

Type	Years	KM#	S#	Y#	X
O13/1939Cyyyy	1939-....	26a	20a	25	

6. O17/ ½ Franken (CHF 0.50)

The Franken was introduced in 1850 as equal to the French Franc. That would mean that the weight of the Franken coin would be 5 grams and consist of 90% silver. As a result the ½ Franken coin would be 2.5 grams of 90% silver. Following the foundation of the Latin Monetary Union between France, Belgium, Italy and Switzerland it was agreed that the smaller silver coins (½, 1 and 2 Franken) would get a fineness of 83.5% silver. Although the LMU was abolished after World War I the Swiss silver coins continued to be issued in 83.5% silver until silver prices rose above face value during the late 1960s. The composition of these coins was then changed to copper-nickel (equal to the smaller 5, 10 and 20 rappen coins) in 1968. As a result three different ½ Franken coin series were issued in Switzerland.

Series	Years	Comp.	Mass (g)	Size (mm)	THK (mm)
O17/1850C	1850-1851	Silver (90% Ag, 10% Cu)	2.5	18.20	0.9
O17/1875C	1875-1967	Silver (83.5% Ag, 16.5% Cu)	2.5	18.20	0.9
O17/1968C	1968-....	Copper-nickel (75% Cu, 25% Ni)	2.2	18.20	0.9

6.1. O17/1850C 90% silver ½ Franken coin (1850-1851)

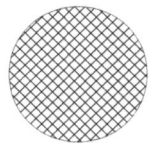

Only minted in 1850 and 1851 in one design that is the same as for the 1, 2 and 5 Franken coins in this period.

Obverse: Sitting lady with "HELVETIA" above.

Reverse: "½ Fr." above mintage year with wreath around. The designs are equal to the 1 and 5 Franken coins depicted later. The 90% silver coins (except the 5 Franken) were demonetised on 1 January 1869.

Type	Years	KM#	S#	Y#	X
O17/1850Cyyyy	1850-1851	8	20	26	

6.2. O17/1875C 83.5% silver ½ Franken coin (1875-1967)

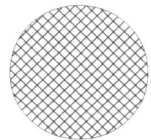

Issued according to Latin Monetary Union standards. Unlike all other coins according to this standard from other countries these coins survived World War I and were issued until 1967, and demonetised on 1 April 1971. Just like most other Swiss coins issued since 1875 this series has one design only.

Obverse   *Reverse*

Obverse: Standing lady with Swiss shield to the right.

Reverse: "½ Fr." above mintage year with wreath around.

Type	Years	KM#	S#	Y#	X
O17/1875Cyyyy	1875-1967	23	27	30	

6.3. O17/1968C Copper-nickel ½ Franken coin (1968-....)

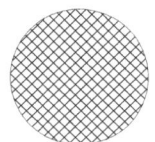

Issued since 1968 because the silver price rose above the face value of these coins. Only one design, which is the same as the former (O17/1875C). However, the number of stars on the obverse increased by one in 1983. The number of stars represent the number of cantons of Switzerland and in 1983 this increased by one due to the creation of the new canton Jura in 1979. Until 1981 these coins were minted in coin alignment (obverse and reverse were minted upside-down relative to each other), from 1982 they were minted in medal alignment (obverse and reverse were minted rightside-up to each other).

| Obverse A¹ | Obverse A² | Reverse A |

Obverse A¹: Standing lady with Swiss shield to the right. 22 stars around the figure.

Obverse A²: As obverse A¹ but with 23 stars.

Reverse A: "½ Fr." above mintage year with wreath around.

Type	Years	KM#	S#	Y#	X
O17/1968CyyyyA¹A	1968-1982	23a.1; 23a.2*	27a.1; 27a.2		
O17/1968CyyyyA²A	1983-....	23a.3	57		

*Version a.1 is minted in coin alignment, a.2 in medal alignment.

7. O20/ 1 Franken (CHF 1.00)

The Franken was introduced in 1850 as the monetary unit of Switzerland with a value and composition equal to the French Franc. That would mean that the weight of the Franken coin would be 5 grams and would consist of 90% silver. In 1860 the fineness was reduced to 80% silver. Following the foundation of the Latin Monetary Union between France, Belgium, Italy and Switzerland it was agreed that the smaller silver coins (½, 1 and 2 Franken) would have a fineness of 83.5% silver. Although the Latin Monetary Union was abolished after World War I the Swiss silver coins continued to be issued in 83.5% silver until silver prices rose above face value during the late 1960s. The composition of these coins was then changed to copper-nickel (equal to the smaller 5, 10 and 20 rappen coins) in 1968. As a result four different 1 Franken coin series were issued in Switzerland.

Series	Years	Comp.	Mass (g)	Size (mm)	THK (mm)
O20/1850C	1850-1857	Silver (90% Ag, 10% Cu)	5.0	23.2	1.1
O20/1860C	1860-1861	Silver (80% Ag, 20% Cu)	5.0	23.2	1.1
O20/1875C	1875-1967	Silver (83.5% Ag, 16.5% Cu)	5.0	23.2	1.1
O20/1968C	1968-....	Copper-nickel (75% Cu, 25% Ni)	4.4	23.2	1.2

7.1. O20/1850C 90% silver 1 Franken coin (1850-1857)

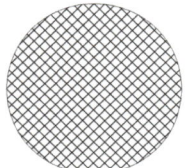

Minted in 1850, 1851 and 1857. Only one design that is the same as for O20/1860C. These coins were demonetised on 1 January 1869.

Obverse: Sitting lady with "HELVETIA" above.

Reverse: "1 Fr." above mintage year with wreath around.

Type	Years	KM#	S#	Y#	X
O20/1850Cyyyy	1850-1857	9	21	27	

7.2. O20/1860C 80% silver 1 Franken coin (1860-1861)

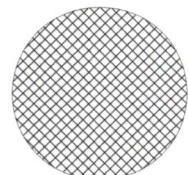

Minted in 1860 and 1861 with the same design as O20/1850C. The coins of this series were demonetised on 1 January 1878.

Obverse   *Reverse*

Obverse: Sitting lady with "HELVETIA" above.

Reverse: "1 Fr." above mintage year with wreath around.

Type	Years	KM#	S#	Y#	X
O20/1860Cyyyy	1860-1861	9a	21a	27	

7.3. O20/1875C 83.5% silver 1 Franken coin (1875-1967)

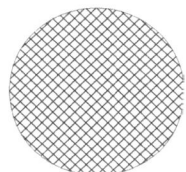

Issued according to Latin Monetary Union standards. Unlike the coins issued according to this standard from other countries these coins survived World War I and were issued until 1967 and demonetised on 1 April 1971. Just like most other Swiss coins issued since 1875 this series has one design only.

Obverse   *Reverse*

Obverse: Standing lady with Swiss shield to the right.

Reverse: "1 Fr." above mintage year with wreath around.

Type	Years	KM#	S#	Y#	X
O20/1875Cyyyy	1875-1967	24	28	31	

7.4. O20/1968C Copper-nickel 1 Franken coin (1968-....)

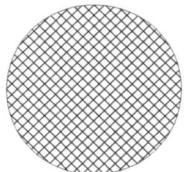

Issued since 1968 because the silver price rose above the face value of these coins. Only one design, which is the same as the former (O20/1875C). However, the number of stars on the obverse increased from 22 to 23 in 1983. Until 1981 these coins were minted in coin alignment (obverse and reverse were minted upside-down relative to each other), from 1982 they were minted in medal alignment (obverse and reverse were minted rightside-up to each other).

Obverse A¹   *Obverse A²*   *Reverse A*

Obverse A¹: Standing lady with Swiss shield to the right. 22 stars around the figure.

Obverse A²: As obverse A¹ but with 23 stars.

Reverse A: "1 Fr." above mintage year with wreath around.

Type	Years	KM#	S#	Y#	X
O17/1968CyyyyA¹A	1968-1982	23a.1; 23a.2*	27a.1; 27a.2		
O17/1968CyyyyA²A	1983-....	23a.3	57		

*Version a.1 is minted in coin alignment, a.2 in medal alignment.

8. O23/ 2 Franken (CHF 2.00)

The Franken was introduced in 1850 as equal to the French Franc. That indicates that the weight of the 2 Franken coin is 10 grams and consist of 90% silver. In 1860 the fineness was reduced to 80% silver. Following the foundation of the Latin Monetary Union between France, Belgium, Italy and Switzerland it was agreed that the smaller silver coins (½, 1 and 2 Franken) have a fineness of 83.5% silver. Although the Latin Monetary Union was abolished after World War I the Swiss silver coins continued to be issued in 83.5% silver until silver prices rose above face value during the late 1960s. The composition of these coins was then changed to copper-nickel (equal to the smaller 5, 10 and 20 rappen coins) in 1968. As a result four different 2 Franken coin series were issued in Switzerland.

Series	Years	Comp.	Mass (g)	Size (mm)	THK (mm)
O23/1850C	1850-1857	Silver (90% Ag, 10% Cu)	10.0	27.4	1.6
O20/1860C	1860-1863	Silver (80% Ag, 20% Cu)	10.0	27.4	1.6
O23/1874C	1874-1967	Silver (83.5% Ag, 16.5% Cu)	10.0	27.4	1.6
O23/1968C	1968-....	Copper-nickel (75% Cu, 25% Ni)	8.8	27.4	1.7

8.1. O23/1850C 90% silver 2 Franken coin (1850-1857)

Minted in 1850 and 1857. Only one design, equal to O20/1850C but with "2 Fr.". These coins were demonetised on 1 January 1869.

Obverse: Sitting lady with "HELVETIA" above.

Reverse: "2 Fr." above mintage year with wreath around.

Type	Years	KM#	S#	Y#	X
O23/1850Cyyyy	1850-1857	10	22	28	

8.2. O23/1860C 80% silver 2 Franken coin (1860-1863)

Minted in 1860, 1862 and 1863 with the same design as O23/1850C. The coins of this series were demonetised on 1 January 1878.

Obverse: Sitting lady with "HELVETIA" above.

Reverse: "2 Fr." above mintage year with wreath around.

Type	Years	KM#	S#	Y#	X
O23/1860Cyyyy	1860-1863	10a	22a	28	

8.3. O23/1874C 83.5% silver 2 Franken coin (1874-1967)

Issued according to Latin Monetary Union standards. Unlike the coins issued according to this standard from other countries these coins survived World War I and were issued until 1967 and demonetised on 1 April 1971. Just like most other Swiss coins issued since 1857 this series has one design only.

Obverse   *Reverse*

Obverse: Standing lady with Swiss shield to the right.

Reverse: "2 Fr." above mintage year with wreath around.

Type	Years	KM#	S#	Y#	X
O23/1874Cyyyy	1875-1967	24	28	31	

8.4. O23/1968C Copper-nickel 2 Franken coin (1968-....)

Issued since 1968 because the silver price rose above the face value of these coins. Only one design, which is the same as the former (O23/1874C). However, the number of stars on the obverse increased from 22 to 23 in 1983. Until 1981 these coins were minted in coin alignment (obverse and reverse were minted upside-down relative to each other), from 1982 they were minted in medal alignment (obverse and reverse were minted rightside-up to each other).

Obverse A¹   *Obverse A²*   *Reverse A*

Obverse A¹: Standing lady with Swiss shield to the right. 22 stars around the figure.

Obverse A²: As obverse A¹ but with 23 stars.

Reverse A: "1 Fr." above mintage year with wreath around.

Type	Years	KM#	S#	Y#	X
O17/1968CyyyyA¹A	1968-1982	23a.1; 23a.2*	27a.1; 27a.2		
O17/1968CyyyyA²A	1983-....	23a.3	57		

*Version a.1 is minted in coin alignment, .2 in medal alignment.

9. O27/ 5 Franken (CHF 5.00)

Unlike the smaller valued silver coins the fineness of the 5 Franken coins (and equivalents in other countries) continued to be 90% silver when Switzerland became a member of the Latin Monetary Union. As a result all 5 Franken coins issued between 1850 and 1928 were large coins with a weight of 25 grams and a fineness of 90% silver. In 1931 both the the size and the fineness of the coins was decreased. Together with the lower valued coins they were issued in copper-nickel from 1968, although for one more year, in 1969 it was minted in silver again. The 5 Franken denomination is the lowest denomination that has also been issued as paper money. Originally the lowest value paper money was supposed to be 10 Franken, but due to World War I and the following hoarding of silver coins the introduction of smaller valued 5 Franken notes was made necessary. 5 Franken notes were not only issued by the National Bank, but during World War I also by the Swiss treasury. Both organisations only issued one paper money version of the 5 Franken denomination. The 5 Franken denomination also is the lowest value that has been issued regularly as commemorative coins. Apart from the regular silver and copper-nickel coins composition between 1976 and 1979 a nickel rich variety of the copper-nickel coins was used for commemorative issues and between 1999 and 2003 a bimetallic version was used as for commemorative coins. In total that means that seven coin and paper money series can be distinguished for this denomination, five coin series (of which two were only used for commemorative coins) and two paper money series, one from the Swiss National Bank and one from the Treasury.

Series	Years	Comp.	Mass (g)	Size (mm)	THK (mm)
O27/1850C	1850-1928	Silver (90% Ag, 10% Cu)	25.0	37.0	2.2
O27/1913N	1913-1952	Paper		70x125	
O27/1914N	1914	Paper		74x116	
O27/1931C	1931-1969	Silver (83.5% Cu, 16.5% Cu)	15.0	31.45	1.9
O27/1968C	1968-....	Copper-nickel (75% Cu, 25% Ni)	13.2	31.45	2.35
O27/1976C	1976-1979	Copper-nickel (65% Cu, 35% Ni)	13.2	31.45	2.35
O27/1999C	1999-2003	Bimetallic*	15.0	32.85	2.5

*Outer ring copper-nickel (Cu 75%, Ni 25%), inner disc nordic gold (89% Cu, 5% Al, 5% Zn, 1% Sn) with a diameter of 23.0 mm).

9.1. O27/1850C Large silver 5 Franken coin (1850-1928)

Issued with three different designs. The last of this has two versions of the reverse design. The coins of this specification were demonetised on 1 February 1934 after they were replaced by the smaller coins of series O27/1931C. This series has also been used for minting so called "Shooting Festival Commemoratives" between 1855 and 1885. Although these coins were minted according to the same standard as the regular issues they were not given legal tender status. In spite of this the value, "5 Fr.", was indicated on the coins with government consent. As they have the same specifications as regular coins they are incorporated however in most catalogues and they are mentioned here with a separate line in the type species table.

Obverse A   *Obverse B*   *Obverse C*

Obverse A: Sitting lady with "HELVETIA" above. Image from Dye's Coin Encyclopedia.

Obverse B: Female head representing liberty with legend "CONFOEDERATIO HELVETICA" and mintage year around.

Obverse C: Head of shepherd with legend "CONFOEDERATIO HELVETICA" above.

Reverse A   *Reverse B*   *Reverse C[1]*

Reverse A: "5 Fr." above mintage year with wreath around. Image from Dye's Coin Encyclopedia.

Reverse B: Shield of the Swiss coat of Arms with "5" to the left and "F" to the right with wreath around.

Reverse C[1]: Shield of the Swiss coat of Arms with leaves to the left and right. "5 Fr." above.

Reverse C²: As reverse C¹ but denomination as "5 FR.". This design is equal to the designs later used for the smaller 5 Franken coin series O27/1931C and O27/1968C.

Type	Years	KM#	S#	Y#	X
O27/1850CyyyyAA	1850-1874	11	23	29	
O27/1850CyyyyBB	1888-1916	34	30	33	
O27/1850CyyyyCC¹	1922-1923	37	35.1	34	
O27/1850CyyyyCC²	1924-1928	38	35.2	34a	
O27/1850CyyyyZ	1857-1885	Shooting festival commemoratives			

9.2. O27/1913N 2ⁿᵈ banknote series 5 Franken note (1913-1952)

One of the longest running Swiss banknote series. Circulated mostly alongside the silver 5 Franken coins. Considering the relatively small number of silver 5 Franken coins issued the notes were more seen in circulation than the coins. It is important to realise that coins have a much longer lifetime than banknotes. When the 5 Franken notes were discontinued in 1952 the mintage of the 5 Franken coins was increased. These banknotes were issued in one design with various issue dates and three signature varieties per issue date.

Obverse   *Reverse*

Obverse: Portrait of Wilhelm Tell to the right. Value and issuer of note in centre.

Reverse: Large "5" in centre of note.

Type	Date	P# (3rd ed.)	P# (21st cent. ed.)	X
O27/1913Nyyyy	Various dates between 1 August 1913 and 28 March 1952	151	11	

9.3. O27/1914N 5 Franken treasury note

Issued at the start of World War I to replace the silver and gold coins that were hoarded due to war conditions in the countries around Switzerland, that was however not involved in the war. Issued in one design, that was printed in each of the three national languages (German, French or Italian)

Obverse A[1]: Image of Libertas to the right and Winkelried to the left. Value and issuer in German in the centre.

Obverse A[2]: As obverse A[1], but value and issuer in French.

Obverse A[3]: As obverse A[1], but value and issuer in Italian.

Reverse A: Two "5"s to the left and right, value spelled out in the three languages in the centre of the note.

Type	Date	P# (3rd ed.)	P# (21st cent. ed.)	X
O27/1914N1914A[1]A	10 August 1914	154	14	
O27/1914N1914A[2]A	10 August 1914	155	15	
O27/1914N1914A[3]A	10 August 1914	156	16	

9.4. O27/1931C Small silver 5 Franken coin (1931-1969)

Issued with the same design as the last type of O27/1850C. This series has been used for commemorative coins from 1936 until 1963. Unlike the earlier shooting commemoratives these smaller silver commemoratives were given legal tender status for the same value (5 Fr.) as the regular coins. The small silver 5 Franken coins were demonetised on 1 April 1971.

Obverse   *Reverse*

Obverse: Head of shepherd with legend "CONFOEDERATIO HELVETICA" above.

Reverse: Shield of the Swiss coat of Arms with leaves to the left and right. "5 FR." above.

Type	Years	KM#	S#	Y#	X
O27/1931Cyyyy	1931-1969	40	36	36	
O27/1931CyyyyZ	1936-1963	Commemorative designs			

9.5. O27/1968 Copper-nickel 5 Franken coin (1968-....)

Together with the smaller valued coins the 5 Franken coin also changed to copper-nickel in 1968. Only in 1969 these coins were, for just one year, minted in silver again. The reason for this was that because of the lower silver content per Franken in these coins it was not essential that the 5 Franken were made in copper-nickel too. In spite of that they were already minted in copper-nickel in 1968 but not issued. It appeared that silver coins disappeared from circulation quickly, so that after 1969 it was considered not feasible anymore to issue silver 5 Franken coins and it was decided to mint these coins also solely in copper-nickel. Although these coins are issued with one design only, A few varieties can be recognised. From 1968 until 1981 they were issued in coin alignment with raised edge lettering. From 1982 until 1984 they were issued in medal alignment with raised edge lettering. From 1985 until 1993 minted in medal alignment with incuse edge lettering. Since 1994 they are again minted with raised edge lettering. The 5 Franken coins with incuse edge lettering are no longer legal tender (they were demonetised on 1 January 2004), all other copper-nickel 5 Franken are still legal tender. In 1974 and 1975 and from 1980 until 1990 this series was also used to issue 5 Franken commemorative coins.

Obverse   *Reverse*

Obverse: Head   of   shepherd   with   legend
"CONFOEDERATIO HELVETICA" above.

Reverse: Shield of the Swiss coat of Arms with leaves to
the left and right. "5 FR." above.

Type	Years	KM#	S#	Y#	X
O27/1968Cyyyy	1968-....	40a	36a		
O27/1968CyyyyZ	1974-1990	Commemorative designs			

9.6. O27/1976C Copper-nickel 5 Franken coin with increased nickel content (1976-1979)

Issued as four (4) commemorative coins only.

9.7. O27/1999C Bimetallic 5 Franken coin (1999-2003)

Issued as six (6) commemorative coins only.

10. O30/ 10 Franken (CHF 10.00)

The 10 Franken denominations circulated for most of its existence as paper money. Only from 1911 until 1922 it was issued as gold coin for circulation, however, due to World War I these coins did not see wide circulation. Since 2004 this denomination is issued as coin again, but only for commemorative purposes and with relatively small mintages. For the rest this denomination was issued as one treasury note series during World War I and three banknote series issued since 1955.

Series	Years	Comp.	Mass (g)	Size (mm)	THK (mm)
O30/1911C	1911-1922	Gold (90% AU, 10% Cu)	3.23	19.0	0.7
O30/1914N	1914	Paper		85x128	
O30/1955N	1955-1977	Paper		75x137	
O30/1979N	1979-1992	Paper		66x137	
O30/1995N	1995-....	Paper		74x126	
O30/2004C	2004-....	Bimetallic*	15.0	32.85	2.5

*Outer ring aluminium-bronze (92% Cu, 6% Al, 2% Ni), inner disc copper-nickel (75% Cu, 25% Ni) with a diameter of 23.0 mm).

10.1. O30/1911C Gold 10 Franken coin (1911-1922)

This coin was issued as circulation gold coin from just before World War I. Due to thes war it saw only little circulation. Issued in one design only. They were effectively (but not formally) demonetised on 27 September 1936 due to the devaluation of the Swiss Franken on that day.

Obverse   *Reverse*

Obverse: Head of "Vrenelli" with "HELVETIA" at top. Image available from Swissmint website and used by permission. Copyright Swissmint.

Reverse: "Shining" Swiss cross with value and year below. Image available from Swissmint website and used by permission. Copyright Swissmint.

Type	Years	KM#	S#	Y#	X
O30/1911Cyyyy	1911-1922	36	33	42	

10.2. O30/1914N 10 Franken treasury note

Issued at the start of World War I to replace the silver and gold coins that were hoarded due to war conditions in the countries around Switzerland, that was however not involved in the war. Issued in one design, that was printed in each of the three national languages (German, French or Italian)

Obverse A[1]: Image of Libertas to the right and Wilhem Telld to the left. Value and issuer in German in the middle

Obverse A[2]: As obverse A[1], but value and issuer in French.

Obverse A[3]: As obverse A[1], but value and issuer in Italian.

Reverse A: Two "10"s to the left and right, value spelled out in the three languages in the centre of the note.

Type	Date	P# (3rd ed.)	P# (21st cent. ed.)	X
O30/1914N1914A[1]A	10 August 1914	157	17	
O30/1914N1914A[2]A	10 August 1914	158	18	
O30/1914N1914A[3]A	10 August 1914	159	19	

10.3. O30/1955N 5th banknote series 10 Franken note (1955-1977)

Issued with one design with various issue dates and three signature varieties per issue date.

Obverse   *Reverse*

Obverse: Portrait of the poet Gottfried Keller to right.

Reverse: Edelweiss plant with "10" to right.

Type	Dates	P# (3rd ed.)	P# (21st cent. ed.)	X
O30/1955Nyyyy	Various dates between 25 August 1955 and 6 January 1977	174	45	

10.4. O30/1979N 6th banknote series 10 Franken

Issued with one design with various issue years and signature varieties. From this series the year of issue is incorporated in the serial number as the first two digits.

Obverse   *Reverse*

Obverse: The mathematician Leonard Euler (1707-1783) to the right. Printed in orange-brown.

Reverse: Water turbine, light rays and solar system.

Type	Years	P# (3rd ed.)	P# (21st cent. ed.)	X
O30/1979Nyyyy	Issued in various years between 1979 and 1992	174	45	

10.5. O30/1995N 8th banknote series 10 Franken banknote (1995-....)

Issued with one design with various issue years and signature varieties. Since 2000 this note contains the value also as perforated number.

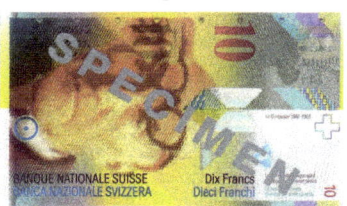

Obverse A¹   *Reverse A*

Obverse A¹: The architect Le Corbusier (1887-1965). Printed in brown-orange.

Obverse A²: As obverse A¹ with perforated numeral "10" below printed numeral "10".

Reverse A: Buildings designed by Le Corbusier.

Type	Years	P# (3ʳᵈ ed.)	P# (21ˢᵗ cent. ed.)	X
O30/1995NyyyyA¹A	Issued in 1995 and 1996		66	
O30/1995NyyyyA²A	Issued since 2000		67	

10.6. O30/2004C Bimetallic 10 Franken coin (1994-....)

Issued as commemorative coins only.

11. O33/ 20 Franken (CHF 20.00)

In the Latin Monetary Union the 20 Franken denomination was the standard denomination for gold coins. As a consequence also Switzerland issued gold 20 Franken coins for several years although the first general issue was only minted in 1883. Apparently before 1883 20 Francs and 20 Lira coins from France and Italy served as the main instrument for larger payments. After the foundation of the Swiss National Bank the first 20 Franken banknotes were issued in 1911 and since then paper money was the main form of this denomination. Only since 1991 20 Franken coins were issued again, but solely for the purpose as commemorative coins. As a result two coin series and six paper money series were issued. Of these six paper money series five were issued by the Swiss National Bank and one, at the start of World War I, by the Swiss treasury.

Series	Years	Comp.	Mass (g)	Size (mm)	THK (mm)
O33/1883C	1883-1949	Gold (90% Au, 10% Cu)	6.45	21.0	1.1
O33/1911N	1911-1929	Paper		95x163	
O33/1914N	1914	Paper		92x145	
O33/1929N	1929-1951	Paper		86x143	
O33/1954N	1954-1976	Paper		85x155	
O33/1978N	1978-1992	Paper		70x148	
O33/1991C	1991-....	Silver (83.5% Ag, 16.5% Cu)	20.0	32.8	2.8
O33/1994N	1994-....	Paper		74x137	

11.1. O33/1883C Gold 20 Franken coin (1883-1949)

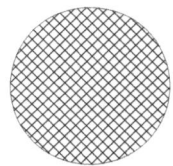

Issued according to Latin Monetary Union standards and as such legal tender in all member countries of this union. Issued in two versions, not counting the proof coins that were issued in small numbers is a few years. They were effectively (but not formally) demonetised on 27 September 1936 due to the devaluation of the Swiss Franken on that day.

Obverse A   *Obverse B*

Obverse A: Female head representing liberty facing left with "CONFOEDERATIO HELVETICA" to left and right. Image available from Swissmint website and used by permission. Copyright Swissmint.

Obverse B: Female head representing "Vrenelli" facing left with "HELVETIA" above.

Reverse A   *Reverse B*

Reverse A: Swiss coat of arms between "20" and "FR" with year below and wreath around. Image available from Swissmint website and used by permission. Copyright Swissmint.

Reverse B: Swiss coat of arms with oak leaves between "20" and "FR" with year below.

Type	Years	KM#	S#	Y#	X
O33/1883CyyyyAA	1883-1896	31	31	40	
O33/1883CyyyyBB	1897-1949	35	32	41	

11.2. O33/1911N 2nd banknote series 20 Franken note (1911-1929)

Issued with one design. However due to changes in the law three subdesigns of the obverse can be recognised.

Each of the date varieties has three different signature varieties.

Obverse A³   *Reverse A*

Obverse A¹: 'Vreneli' (woman's head) in left-hand side medallion. Law from 6 October 1905.

Obverse A²: As obverse A¹ but law from 7 April 1921.

Obverse A³: As obverse A¹ but "Gesetzgebung über die Schweizerische Nationalbank".

Reverse A: Ornaments, rosette, and numeral of value in centre.

Type	Years	P# (3rd ed.)	P# (21st cent. ed.)	X
O33/1911NyyyyA¹A	Various dates between 1 December 1911 and 1 January 1922	150	12	
O33/1911N1922A²A	1 July 1922 only	164	27	
O33/1911NyyyyA³A	Various dates between 1 May 1923 and 18 April 1929	168	33	

11.3. O33/1914N 20 Franken treasury note

Issued at the start of World War I to replace the silver and gold coins that were hoarded due to war conditions in the countries around Switzerland, which was one of the few counties that were not involved in this war. Issued in one design, that was printed in each of the three national languages (German, French or Italian)

Obverse A[1]: Image of Libertas to the right and Winkelried to the left. Value and issuer in German in the middle.

Obverse A[2]: As obverse A[1], but value and issuer in French.

Obverse A[3]: As obverse A[1], but value and issuer in Italian.

Reverse A: Two "10"s to the left and right, value spelled out in the three languages in the centre of the note.

Type	Date	P# (3rd ed.)	P# (21st cent. ed.)	X
O33/1914N1914A[1]A	10 August 1914	160	20	
O33/1914N1914A[2]A	10 August 1914	161	21	
O33/1914N1914A[3]A	10 August 1914	162	22	

11.4. O33/1929N 3rd banknote series 20 Franken note (1929-1951)

Issued with only one design with no subdesigns. Three signature variates for each issue date.

Obverse   Reverse

Obverse: 'Pestalozzi' (Swiss educationalist) in right-hand side medallion. Printed mostly in blue.

Reverse: Swiss cross in the middle of the note.

Type	Date	P# (3rd ed.)	P# (21st cent. ed.)	X
O33/1929Nyyyy	Various dates between 12 June 1929 and 28 March 1952	173	39	

11.5. O33/1954N 5th banknote series 20 Franken note (1954-1976)

Issued with only one design with no subdesigns. Three signature variates for each issue date.

Obverse   *Reverse*

Obverse: General Dufour on the right. Printed in blue.

Reverse: Thistle

Type	Date	P# (3rd ed.)	P# (21st cent. ed.)	X
O33/1954Nyyyy	Various dates between 1 July 1954 and 9 April 1976	175	46	

11.6. O33/1978N 6th banknote series 20 Franken note (1978-1992)

Issued with only one design with two subdesigns. From this series the year of issue is incorporated in the serial number as the first two digits. Three signature variations for each year of issue.

Obverse A¹   *Reverse A*

Obverse A¹: The geologist Horace-Bénédict de Saussure (1740–1799). Wide edge around image.

Obverse A²: As obverse A¹ with small edge around image.

Reverse A: Mountain range, a group of alpinists and the Ammonshorn.

Type	Years	P# (3rd ed.)	P# (21st cent. ed.)	X
O33/1978N1978A¹A	Only issued in 1978	189	54	
O33/1978NyyyyA²A	Various issued years from 1978 until 1992		55	

11.7. O33/1991C Silver 20 Franken coins (1991-....)

Issued as commemorative coins only.

11.8. O33/1994N 8th banknote series 20 Franken note (1994-....)

Issued with only one design with two subdesigns. The year of issue is incorporated in the serial number as the first two digits. Three signature variations for each year of issue.

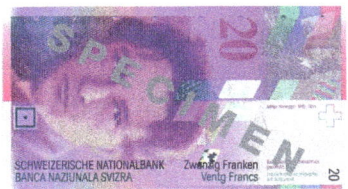

Obverse A¹

Reverse A

Obverse A¹: Arthur Honegger (1892–1955), composer. Printed in red.

Obverse A²: As obverse A¹ with perforated value ("20") below printed value ("20").

Reverse A: The orchestral works: Pacific 231 locomotive, the score and the work instrument.

Type	Years	P# (3rd ed.)	P# (21st cent. ed.)	X
O33/1994NyyyyA¹A	1994 and 1995		68	
O33/1994NyyyyA²A	2000-....		69	

12. O34/ 25 Franken (CHF 25.00)

The 25 Franken denomination is a rare one in Switzerland. It has only been suggested twice, for the first time as a paper money issued by the State Loan Bank of the Swiss Federation (Dahlehnskasse der Schweizerischen Eidgenossenschaft) as emergency issued at the start of World War I, and for the second time as gold coin that was minted in large quantities but in the end was, due to rising gold prices, never issued to the public.

Series	Years	Comp.	Mass (g)	Size (mm)	THK (mm)
O34/1914N	1914	Paper		85x140	
O34/1955C	1955-1959	Gold (90% Au, 10% Cu)	5.645	20.0	1.0

12.1. O34/1914N 25 Franken "Dahrlehnskassenschein"

Issued in 1914 only through the State Loan Bank of the Swiss Federation (in German "Dahrlehnskasse der Schweizerischen Eidgenossenschaft") in order to supply money to a society that hoarded gold and silver coins due to war conditions in the countries surrounding Switzerland.

Obverse A[1]: Swiss cross at centre top, "25" to the left, and upper and lower right. Further ornamental design with serial number outside the yellow field with the value and issueuing authority.

Obverse A[2]: As Obverse A[1] with serial number inside field.

Reverse A: Four "10"s in the corners, value spelled out in the three languages in the centre of the note. Printed in green.

Type	Date	P# (3rd ed.)	P# (21st cent. ed.)	X
O34/1914N1914A¹A	9 September 1914	163	23	
O34/1914N1914A²A	9 September 1914	163	23	

12.2. O34/1955C Gold 25 Franken coin (1955-1959)

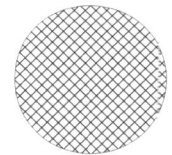

After World War II Switzerland aimed at issuing gold coinage again. As the value of the Franken was decreased since the devaluation on 1936 it was not possible to issue these coins with the old amount of gold, and it was decided to issue lighter coins with values of 25 and 50 Franken. During production of the coins the gold price rose and it was not possible to issue the coins at face value and as according to Swiss law coins could not be issued above face value they were stored in the vaults of the Swiss National Bank where they stayed until 2006. Between 2006 and 2008 almost 98% of these coins were remelted into gold bars (Swissmint, 2009). The rest will stay (for the time being, and perhaps forever) in the SNB vaults.

Obverse   *Reverse*

Obverse: Wilhem Tell.

Reverse: "FR 25" in centre of coin with "CONFOEDERATIO HELVETICA" in legend and mintage year below.

Type	Years	KM#	S#	Y#	X
O34/1955Cyyyy	1955-1959	49	44		

13. O37/ 50 Franken (CHF 50.00)

The 50 Franken was from the foundation of the Swiss National Bank in 1905 a regular banknote denomination, and has solely been issued to the general public in the form of banknotes from the various banknote series. Only during the 1950s there was an attempt to produce gold 50 Franken coins, however, just like the 25 Franken coins these coins could not be issued because of the rising gold prices. Six banknote series have been issued until now.

Series	Years	Comp.	Mass (g)	Size (mm)	THK (mm)
O37/1907N	1907	Paper		103x166	
O37/1910N	1910-1955	Paper		106x165	
O37/1955C	1955-1959*	Gold (90% Au, 10% Cu)	11.29	25.0	1.7
O37/1955N	1955-1974	Paper		95x173	
O37/1978N	1978-1988	Paper		74x159	
O37/1994N	1994-2012	Paper		74x148	

Series	Years	Comp.	Mass (g)	Size (mm)	THK (mm)
O37/2015N	2015-....	Paper		70x137	

*Since 2001 this series is also used to issue gold (proof) coins with very low mintages and at prices perhaps 10 times as high as its face value. These coins are not discussed further in this catalogue.

13.1. O37/1907N 1ˢᵗ banknote series 50 Franken note

Issued after the Swiss National Bank was founded in 1905 with the same design as older notes issued by regional banks. These notes were meant as interim notes that could be issued before the first duly designed SNB notes could be issued. Issued with one date only with three signature varieties.

Obverse   Reverse

Obverse: Portrait of Helvetica to the left.

Reverse: Ornamental design.

Type	Date	P# (3ʳᵈ ed.)	P# (21ˢᵗ cent. ed.)	X
O37/1907N	1 February 1907	142	1	

13.2. O37/1910N 2ⁿᵈ banknote series 50 Franken note (1910-1955)

First regular Swiss 50 Franken banknote. Issued for a long period of 45 years with only one design showing two subdesigns depending on the law that regulates the issuance of these notes. Three signature varieties per date.

Obverse A²   *Reverse A*

Obverse A¹: Woman's head in left-hand side medallion. Issued according to the law of 6 October 1905 ("Gesetz vom 6. Oktober 1905").

Obverse A²: As obverse A¹ but issued according to the law regarding the Swiss National Bank ("Gesetzgebung über die Schweizerische Nationalbank").

Reverse A: Woodcutter.

Type	Date	P# (3rd ed.)	P# (21st cent. ed.)	X
O37/1910NyyyyA¹A	Issued with various dates between 1 January 1910 and 1 August 1920	146	5	
O37/1910NyyyyA²A	Issued with various dates between 1 January 1924 and 29 December 1955	169	34	

13.3. O37/1955C Gold 50 Franken coin (1955-1959)

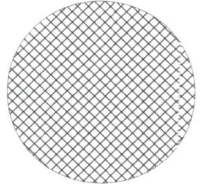

After World War II Switzerland aimed at issuing gold coinage again. As the value of the Franken relative to gold was decreased due to the devaluation of 1936 it was not possible to issue these coins with the same weight of the old gold coins, and it was decided to issue lighter coins with values of 25 and 50 Franken. During production of the coins the gold price rose and it was not possible to issue the coins for circulation as according to Swiss law coins could not be issued above face value. Since then they were stored in the vaults of the Swiss National Bank where they stayed until 2006. Between 2006 and 2008 almost 98% of these coins were remelted into gold bars (Swissmint, 2009). The rest will stay (for the time being, and perhaps forever) in the SNB vaults.

Obverse   *Reverse*

Obverse: Three men representative for the original three cantons of Switzerland.

Reverse: "FR 50" in centre of coin with "CONFOEDERATIO HELVETICA" around and mintage year below.

Type	Years	KM#	S#	Y#	X
O37/1955Cyyyy	1955-1959	50	45		

13.4. O37/1955N 5th banknote series 50 Franken note (1955-1974)

Issued with only one design. Although no subdesigns can be recognised this note is printed at two different printers, which is reflected in the classification of the obverse type. Three signature variates for each issue date.

Obverse A²   *Reverse*

Obverse A¹: Girl's head on the right. Printed at Waterlow & Sons Ltd., London. Printed in green.

Obverse A²: As obverse A¹ but printed at De la Rue, London.

Reverse: Apple harvest.

Type	Date	P# (3rd ed.)	P# (21st cent. ed.)	X
O37/1955NyyyyA¹A	Various dates between 7 July 1955 and 18 December 1958	176a	47	
O37/1955NyyyyA²A	Various dates between 4 May 1961 and 7 February 1974	176b	48	

13.5. O37/1978N 6th banknote series 50 Franken note (1978-1988)

Issued with only one design. From this series the year of issue is incorporated in the serial number as the first two digits. Three signature variations for each year of issue.

Obverse   *Reverse*

Obverse: Konrad Gessner (1516–1565), universal scholar.

Reverse: Eagle owl, primula, stars.

Type	Years	P# (3rd ed.)	P# (21st cent. ed.)	X
O37/1978Nyyyy	Issued in various years from 1978 until 1988	188	56	

13.6. O37/1994N 8th banknote series 50 Franken note (1994-2012)

Issued with only one design with two subdesigns. The year of issue is incorporated in the serial number as the first two digits. Three signature variations for each year of issue.

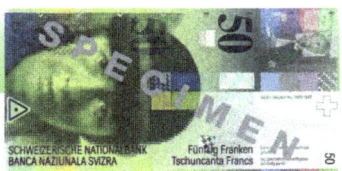 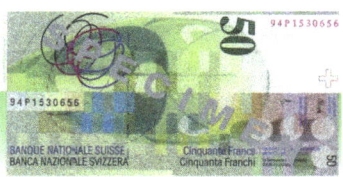

Obverse A¹   *Reverse A*

Obverse A¹: Sophie Täuber-Arp (1889–1943), painter, handcraftswoman, sculptor. Printed in green.

Obverse A²: As obverse A¹ with perforated value ("50") below printed value ("50").

Reverse A: Relief rectangulaire, Tête Dada, Composition Aubette, Lignes ouvertes.

Type	Years	P# (3ʳᵈ ed.)	P# (21ˢᵗ cent. ed.)	X
O37/1994N1994A¹A	1994		70	
O33/1994NyyyyA²A	2000-2012		71	

13.7. O37/2015N 9ᵗʰ banknote series 50 Franken note (2015-....)

Issued for circulation in 2016. Thee signature variations.

Obverse   *Reverse*

Obverse: Design inspired by "wind". Printed in green.

Reverse: Design inspired by "wind".

Type	Years	P# (3ʳᵈ ed.)	P# (21ˢᵗ cent. ed.)	X
O37/2015Nyyyy	First year of printing 2015			

14. O40/ 100 Franken (CHF 100.00)

Issued as six banknote series and one gold coin series. The coins series, issued in one year only had a very small mintage number. Recent gold 100 Franken coins, issued well above face value are not discussed in this catalogue.

Series	Years	Comp.	Mass (g)	Size (mm)	THK (mm)
O40/1907N	1907	Paper		116x183	
O40/1910N	1910-1949	Paper		115x181	
O40/1918N	1918	Paper		115x180	
O40/1925C	1925	Gold (90% Au, 10% Cu)	32.258	35.0	2.0
O40/1956N	1956-1973	Paper		105x191	
O40/1975N	1975-1993	Paper		78x170	
O40/1996N	1996-....	Paper		74x159	

14.1. O40/1907N 1st banknote series 100 Franken note

Issued after the Swiss National Bank was founded in 1905 with the same design as older notes that were issued by regional banks. These notes were meant as interim notes that could be issued before the first duly designed SNB notes could be issued. Issued with one date only with three signature varieties.

Obverse   *Reverse*

Obverse: Portrait of Helvetica to the left.

Reverse: Ornamental design.

Type	Date	P# (3rd ed.)	P# (21st cent. ed.)	X
O40/1907N	1 February 1907	143	2	

14.2. O40/1910N 2nd banknote series 100 Franken note (1910-1949)

First regular Swiss 100 Franken banknote. Issued for a long period of 39 years with only one design showing three subdesigns depending on the law that regulates the issuance of these notes. Three signature variations per date.

Obverse A³   *Reverse*

Obverse A¹: Woman's head in left-hand side medallion. Issued according to the law of 6 October 1905 ("Gesetz vom 6. Oktober 1905"). Printed in dark blue.

Obverse A²: As obverse A¹ but law from 7 April 1921 ("Gesetz vom 7. April 1921")..

Obverse A³: As obverse A¹ but issued according to the law regarding the Swiss National Bank ("Gesetzgebung über die Schweizerische Nationalbank").

Reverse A: Mower (reaper).

Type	Dates	P# (3rd ed.)	P# (21st cent. ed.)	X
O40/1910NyyyyA¹A	Various dates between 1 January 1910 and 1 August 1920	147	6	
O40/1910N1923A²A	1 January 1923 only	165	28	
O40/1910NyyyyA³A	Various dates between 1 April 1924 and 20	170	35	

Type	Dates	P# (3rd ed.)	P# (21st cent. ed.)	X
	January 1949			

14.3. O40/1918N 3rd banknote series 100 Franken note

Issued only in 1918 with two series of notes in one design.

Obverse   *Reverse*

Obverse: William Tell in left-hand side medallion. Printed in brown and blue.

Reverse: Ornaments, rosette, and Jungfrau massif.

Type	Date	P# (3rd ed.)	P# (21st cent. ed.)	X
O40/1918N	1 January 1918	152	9	

14.4. O40/1925C Gold 100 Franken coin

Issued when, after World War I, the gold standard could be fully restored again. It was issued as a coin that was actually meant to be given as present to commemorate this event and considering its very small mintage of only 5000 pieces it did not really circulate as for that purpose the banknotes served as a better alternative.

Obverse   *Reverse*

Obverse: Head of "Vrenelli" with "HELVETIA" at top.

Reverse: "Shining" Swiss cross with value and year below.

Type	Years	KM#	S#	Y#	X
O40/1925Cyyyy	1925	34	39	43	

14.5. O40/1956N 5th banknote series 100 Franken note (1956-1973)

Issued with only one design with no subdesigns. Three signature variates for each issue date.

Obverse   *Reverse*

Obverse: Boy's head on the right. Printed in dark blue.

Reverse: St. Martin.

Type	Date	P# (3rd ed.)	P# (21st cent. ed.)	X
O40/1965Nyyyy	Various dates between 25 October 1956 and 7 March 1973	177	49	

14.6. O40/1975N 6ᵗʰ banknote series 100 Franken note (1975-1993)

Issued with only one design. From this series the year of issue is incorporated in the serial number as the first two digits. Three signature variations for each year of issue.

Obverse *Reverse*

Obverse: Francesco Borromini (1599–1667), architect. Printed in blue.

Reverse: Upper part of the dome-tower as well as the floor plan of the church Saint Ivo.

Type	Years	P# (3ʳᵈ ed.)	P# (21ˢᵗ cent. ed.)	X
O40/1975Nyyyy	Issued in various years from 1975 until 1993	188	56	

14.7. O40/1996N 8ᵗʰ banknote series 100 Franken note (1996-....)

Issued with only one design. The year of issue is incorporated in the serial number as the first two digits. Three signature variations for each year of issue.

Obverse *Reverse*

Obverse: Alberto Giacometti (1901–1966), sculptor, painter. Printed in blue.

Reverse: Lotar ll, homme qui marche and time-space relationship, works by Giacometti.

Type	Years	P# (3rd ed.)	P# (21st cent. ed.)	X
O40/1996Nyyyy	Various years from 1996 until now		72	

15. O43/ 200 Franken (CHF 200.00)

The 200 Franken denomination has been introduced for the first time in the 8th banknote series as replacement of the 500 Franken note that was discontinued from that series.

Series	Years	Comp.	Mass (g)	Size (mm)	THK (mm)
O43/1996N	1996-....	Paper		74x170	

15.1. O43/1996N 8th banknote series 200 Franken note (1996-....)

Issued with only one design. The year of issue is incorporated in the serial number as the first two digits. Three signature variations for each year of issue.

Obverse   *Reverse*

Obverse: Charles Ferdinand Ramuz (1878–1947), writer. Printed in brown.

Reverse: The mountain world, the lake, the manuscript.

Type	Years	P# (3rd ed.)	P# (21st cent. ed.)	X
O43/1996Nyyyy	Various years from 1996 until now		73	

16. O44/ 250 Franken (CHF 250.00)

This denomination has only been used to issue a commemorative coin in fairly large numbers to commemorate the 700th birthday of the Swiss Confederation.

Series	Years	Comp.	Mass (g)	Size (mm)	THK (mm)
O44/1991C	1991	Gold (90% Au, 10% Cu)	8.0	23.0	1.5

16.1. O44/1991C Gold 250 Franken coin

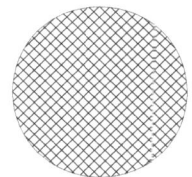

Used to issue (only) one commemorative coin, to celebrate the 700th anniversary of the Swiss Confederation. This coin series has been mentioned here as this coin was produced in large numbers and issued at face value.

17. O47/ 500 Franken (CHF 500.00)

The denomination 500 Franken was a common banknote denomination until the 6th banknote series. It was no longer issued in the 8th banknote series, when it was replaced with the 200 Franken note. This denomination has been issued in four banknote series only and never as coins.

Series	Years	Comp.	Mass (g)	Size (mm)	THK (mm)
O40/1907N	1907	Paper		116x183	
O40/1910N	1910-1949	Paper		115x181	
O40/1956N	1956-1973	Paper		105x191	
O40/1975N	1975-1993	Paper		78x170	

17.1. O47/1907N 1st banknote series 500 Franken note

Issued after the Swiss National Bank was founded in 1905 with the same design as older notes that were issued by regional banks. These notes were meant as interim notes that could be issued before the first duly designed SNB notes could be issued. Issued with one date only with three signature varieties.

Obverse   *Reverse*

Obverse: Portrait of Helvetica to the left. Printed in green.

Reverse: Ornamental design.

Type	Date	P# (3rd ed.)	P# (21st cent. ed.)	X
O47/1907N	1 February 1907	144	3	

17.2. O47/1910N 2nd banknote series 500 Franken note (1910-1947)

First regular Swiss 500 Franken banknote. Issued for a long period of 37 years with only one design showing three subdesigns depending on the law that regulates the issuance of these notes. Three signature variations per date.

Obverse A³   *Reverse A*

Obverse A¹: Woman's head in left-hand side medallion. Issued according to the law of 6 October 1905 ("Gesetz vom 6. Oktober 1905"). Printed in red and brown.

Obverse A²: As obverse A¹ but law from 7 April 1921 ("Gesetz vom 7. April 1921").

Obverse A³: As obverse A¹ but issued according to the law regarding the Swiss National Bank ("Gesetzgebung über die Schweizerische Nationalbank").

Reverse A: Embroiderers.

Type	Dates	P# (3rd ed.)	P# (21st cent. ed.)	X
O47/1910NyyyyA¹A	Various dates between 1 January 1910 and 1 January 1917	148	7	
O47/1910N1923A²A	1 January 1923 only	166	29	
O47/1910NyyyyA³A	Various dates between 4 October 1928 and 16 October 1947	171	36	

17.3. O47/1957N 5th banknote series 500 Franken note (1957-1974)

Issued with only one design with no subdesigns, but printed at two different facilities. Three signature variates for each issue date.

Obverse A²   *Reverse A*

Obverse A¹: Woman's head on the right. Printed at Waterlow & Sons Ltd., London. Printed in reddish brown.

Obverse A²: As obverse A¹ but printed at De la Rue, London.

Reverse: Fountain of youth.

Type	Date	P# (3rd ed.)	P# (21st cent. ed.)	X
O47/1957NyyyyA¹A	Various dates between 31 January 1957 and 18 December 1958	178a	50	
O47/1957NyyyyA²A	Various dates between 21 December 1961 and 7 February 1974	178b	51	

17.4. O47/1976N 6th banknote series 500 Franken note (1976-1992)

Issued with only one design. From this series the year of issue is incorporated in the serial number as the first two digits. Three signature variations for each year of issue. This was the last 500 Franken note printed and issued. Replaced with a 200 Franken note starting the 8th banknote series.

Obverse	*Reverse*

Obverse: Albrecht von Haller (1708–1777), physician, naturalist and poet. Printed in brown.

Reverse: Muscular figure of a human body, graph of respiration and the circulation of the blood, and a purple orchis.

Type	Years	P# (3rd ed.)	P# (21st cent. ed.)	X
O47/1976Nyyyy	Issued in 1976, 1986 and 1992	186	58	

18. O50/ 1000 Franken (CHF 1000.00)

1000 Franken has always been the largest denomination in Switzerland. These notes were issued from the first series of banknotes and are currently still issued in Switzerland. The current note is the most valuable banknote that is still printed and issued to the general public worldwide after the Monetary Authority of Singapore had decided to stop printing and issuing the 10000 Singapore Dollar banknote in 2014. A total of five banknote 1000 Franken series were issued in Switzerland. They were issued in the 1st, 2nd, 5th, 6th and 8th banknote series. No 1000 Franken note was printed for the 3rd series, and the 4th and 7th series only contained reserve notes that never circulated and as such are not incorporated in this catalogue. The 1000 Franken note of the 9th series has not been issued yet, but will be somewhere in the next few years.

Series	Years	Comp.	Mass (g)	Size (mm)	THK (mm)
O50/1907N	1907	Paper		132x215	
O50/1910N	1910-1955	Paper		131x216	
O50/1954N	1954-1974	Paper		125x228	
O50/1977N	1977-1993	Paper		86x192	
O50/1996N	1996-....	Paper		1996-....	

18.1. O50/1907N 1st banknote series 1000 Franken note

Issued after the Swiss National Bank was founded in 1905 with the same design as older notes that were issued by regional banks. These notes were meant as interim notes that could be issued before the first duly designed SNB notes could be issued. Issued with one date only with three signature varieties.

Obverse   *Reverse*

Obverse: Portrait of Helvetica to the left. Printed in purple and blue.

Reverse: Ornamental design.

Type	Date	P# (3rd ed.)	P# (21st cent. ed.)	X
O50/1907N	1 February 1907	145	4	

18.2. O50/1910N 2nd banknote series 1000 Franken note (1910-1955)

First regular Swiss 1000 Franken banknote. Issued for a long period of 45 years with only one design showing three subdesigns depending on the law that regulates the issuance of these notes. Three signature variations per date.

 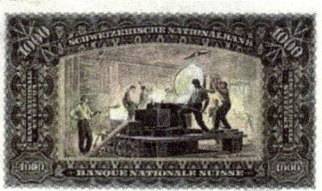

Obverse A³   *Reverse A*

Obverse A¹: Woman's head in left-hand side medallion. Issued according to the law of 6 October 1905 ("Gesetz vom 6. Oktober 1905"). Printed in purple and orange.

Obverse A²: As obverse A¹ but law from 7 April 1921 ("Gesetz vom 7. April 1921").

Obverse A³: As obverse A¹ but issued according to the law regarding the Swiss National Bank ("Gesetzgebung über die Schweizerische Nationalbank").

Reverse A: Embroiderers.

Type	Dates	P# (3rd ed.)	P# (21st cent. ed.)	X
O50/1910NyyyyA¹A	Various dates between 1 January 1910 and 1 January 1917	149	8	
O50/1910N1923A²A	1 January 1923 only	167	30	
O50/1910NyyyyA³A	Various dates between 23 November 1927 and 29 April 1955	172	37	

18.3. O50/1954N 5th banknote series 1000 Franken note (1954-1974)

Issued with only one design with no subdesigns. Three signature variates for each issue date.

Obverse   *Reverse*

Obverse: Woman's head on the right. Printed in purple.

Reverse: Danse macabre.

Type	Date	P# (3rd ed.)	P# (21st cent. ed.)	X
O47/1957Nyyyy	Various dates between 30 September 1954 and 7 February 1974	179	52	

18.4. O50/1977N 6th banknote series 1000 Franken note (1977-1993)

Issued with only one design. From this series the year of issue is incorporated in the serial number as the first two digits. Three signature variations for each year of issue.

Obverse   *Reverse*

Obverse: Auguste Forel (1848-1931), psychiatrist, neurologist, entomologist. Printed in purple.

Reverse: Three ants and a cross-section of an anthill.

Type	Years	P# (3rd ed.)	P# (21st cent. ed.)	X
O50/1976Nyyyy	Issued in 1977, 1980, 1984, 1987, 1988 and 1993	187	59	

18.5. O50/1996N 8th banknote series 1000 Franken note (1996-....)

Issued with only one design. The year of issue is incorporated in the serial number as the first two digits. Three signature variations for each year of issue.

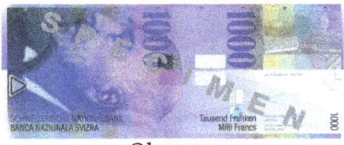 

Obverse   *Reverse*

Obverse: Jacob Burckhardt (1818–1897), historian of art and culture. Printed in purple.

Reverse: Antiquity, ancient architecture, the renaissance, the view of history.

Type	Years	P# (3rd ed.)	P# (21st cent. ed.)	X
O50/1996Nyyyy	Issued in 1996, 1999, 2006 and 2012		74	

Literature

CIA (2014) The World Factbook; Switzerland; available at: https://www.cia.gov/library/publications/the-world-factbook/geos/sz.html [accessed 16th May 2016].

Cuhaj GS (2010) Standard catalog of world paper money. Volume 3. Modern issues 1961-date. 16th edition. Krause Publications Inc, Iola, WI.

Divo JP (1978) Die Münzen de Schweiz und des Fürstentums Liechtenstein. Preiskatalog 1978. 5. Auflage. Kricheldorf Verlag, Freiburg im Breisgau.

Dye JS (1883) Dye's coin encyclopedia: A complete illustrated history of the coins of the world. Available from the Internet Archive at https://archive.org/details/dyescoinencyclop00dyejiala.

Krause CL & Mishler C (1998) 1999 standard catalog of World coins. 26th edition. Krause Publications, Inc, Iola, WI.

Krause CL & Mishler C (1999) Standard catalog of World coins. 1801-1900. 2nd edition. Krause Publications, Inc, Iola, WI.

Müller J. Website "Schweizer Geld" http://www.schweizer-geld.ch/index.php. Visited 9 May 2016.

Schön G & Schön G (2014) Welmunzkatalog 20. & 21. Jahrhundert. 42. Aulage. Battenberg Verlag.

Schweizerische Nationalbank. Website "All SNB banknote series": http://www.snb.ch/en/iabout/cash/history/id/cash_history_overview. Visited 9 May 2016.

Shafer N & Cuhaj GS (2003) Standard catalog of world paper money. Volume 3. Modern issues 1961-date. Krause Publications Inc, Iola, WI.

Swissmint (2008a) Paul Burkhard und der Fünfliber; Prägevarianten 5Fr. Kleinformat. Available from http://www.swissmint.ch/d/downloads/dokumentation/numis_beri/5FR-BURK.pdf.

Swissmint (2008b) DOMINUS PROVIDEBIT / Sterne auf Schweizer Münzen. Available from: http://www.swissmint.ch/d/downloads/dokumentation/numis_beri/Dominus.pdf.

Swissmint (2008c) Das Goldvreneli. Available from: http://www.swissmint.ch/d/downloads/dokumentation/num is_beri/VRENELI.pdf.

Swissmint (2009) Goldmünzen zu 25- und 50-Franken. Available from http://www.swissmint.ch/d/downloads/dokumentation/num is_beri/25-50-FR-GOLDMUENZEN.pdf.

Swissmint (2016) Prägetabelle 2016. Available from: http://www.swissmint.ch/d/downloads/dokumentation/prae geprog/PRAEGELISTE%E2%80%932016.pdf.

Yeoman RS (2008) A catalog of modern World coins 1850-1964. 14th edition. Whitman Publishing LLC, Atlanta GA.